Travel Guide to Bogotá

Unveiling the Best of Columbia's Top City (2024))

Tania Clark

Table of Content

Welcome to Bogotá

The Vibrant Capital of Colombia!

Rain lashed against the cobblestones, each dropping a tiny hammer pounding an urgent rhythm on the ancient city. Elena, cloak plastered to her back, huddled beneath the awning of a shuttered bookstore. She wasn't afraid of the storm; fear had become a distant ember in her eyes. No, what chilled her was the parchment clutched in her clammy hand, the ink bleeding into a crimson stain under the relentless downpour. It was a summons, a whisper on the wind that had summoned her back to the secrets woven into the very fabric of Bogotá.

Elena wasn't born of this rain-swept city, but it embraced her with a bittersweet kiss the day she stumbled upon a hidden chamber beneath the National Museum. Inside, a forgotten library whispered tales of a hidden lineage, of magic tethered to forgotten bloodlines. She was a descendant of the Chorro de Quevedo witches, women who tamed flames and spoke with the ghosts of the colonial past. And now, the whispers had turned to screams, urging her to unravel a conspiracy that threatened to unravel the tapestry of time itself.

The bookstore door creaked open, a beacon of yellow light slicing through the storm. An old woman, eyes the color of moss under a woven shawl, beckoned her inside. Elena stepped across the threshold, the world outside fading into a watercolor canvas. Shelves groaned under the weight of leather-bound secrets, the air thick with the scent of aged paper and forgotten spells. The woman chuckled, a dry rasp like wind through reeds. "Welcome, child of fire," she rasped, "the storm has brought you home."

Elena clutched the summons, the ink staining her fingers a deep, pulsing red. "I don't know what awaits me," she whispered, her voice swallowed by the whispering shelves. "But the city calls, and I must answer." The woman smiled, a flash of lightning between her wrinkled lips. "The city speaks to those who listen," she murmured, "and tonight, it will show you the shadows that dance beneath its emerald heart."

With that, the bookstore swallowed Elena whole, and the storm howled on, a chorus for the secrets about to be unearthed. Her journey had just begun, a dance with destiny played out on the rain-slicked stage of Bogotá, where magic and mayhem waltzed to the rhythm of a thousand unseen hearts.

Bogotá, nestled high in the Colombian Andes, is a pulsating heartbeat at the center of a nation reborn. It's a city bursting with contradictions, where colonial grandeur brushes shoulders with sleek skyscrapers, and street art explodes from crumbling walls. It's a place where ancient rituals whisper under the shadow of modern towers, and where the aroma of fresh tamales dances with the scent of trendy craft brews.

Forget the tired stereotypes of the past. This Bogotá is an adrenaline rush for the senses, a kaleidoscope of experiences waiting to be devoured. It's a city that reinvents itself daily, where you can salsa under the stars one night and sip craft cocktails in a rooftop bar overlooking the sprawling cityscape the next.

Beyond the cobblestone streets of La Candelaria, where colonial churches whisper tales of conquistadors and revolutionaries, a new Bogotá takes flight. Zona Rosa, with its glittering facades and designer boutiques, caters to the high-rollers, while Macarena, the bohemian enclave, pulsates with independent art galleries, trendy cafes, and rooftop bars spilling onto the streets. In Chapinero, you'll find co-working spaces buzzing with tech startups, alongside traditional craft breweries and live music venues. In Usaquén, families picnic in manicured parks, browsing upscale boutiques and gourmet markets.

Bogotá's heart beats to the rhythm of its people. Warm smiles greet you on every corner, and the infectious energy of locals spills from sidewalk cafes and salsa clubs. Immerse yourself in the vibrant rhythm of street vendors hawking exotic fruits and hot arepas, and let the infectious laughter of children playing in bustling plazas wash over you.

But Bogotá is a city steeped in history, too. The Gold Museum glitters with pre-Columbian treasures, each artifact a silent guardian of forgotten empires. Climb the Monserrate mountain for panoramic vistas and a colonial church that whispers of conquistadors and prayers. Explore the Botero Museum, where Fernando Botero's rotund sculptures distort reality and tickle your funny bone in equal measure.

And then there's the food. Bogotá is a foodie paradise, where traditional Colombian staples like ajiaco (chicken stew) and bandeja paisa (a meat-and-bean feast) tempt your tastebuds. Venture beyond the familiar, though, and discover a city bursting with international flavors. Sushi restaurants rub shoulders with Italian trattorias, and Peruvian ceviche stands to fight for sidewalk space with trendy vegan cafes.

But this is a city that lives after dark, too. Salsa clubs pulsate with the city's heartbeat, as couples twirl under flashing lights. Rooftops transform into open-air bars, buzzing with conversations and laughter. Live music spills out of smoky jazz clubs, and hidden speakeasies offer cocktails crafted with artisanal spirits.

Beyond the city limits, adventure awaits. Day trips to nearby towns like Zipaquirá (with its breathtaking salt cathedral carved into the earth) and Guatavita (a sacred lake shimmering like an emerald in the mountains) offer a glimpse into Colombia's rich history and stunning natural beauty. Venture farther afield to the lush green embrace of the Coffee Region, where you can learn the secrets of the perfect cup and immerse yourself in the vibrant culture of Colombia's campesinos. Or, for the truly adventurous, embark on an unforgettable journey into the Amazon rainforest, where the symphony of the jungle replaces the city's hum and ancient secrets lie hidden beneath the emerald canopy.

Planning your Bogotá adventure is effortless. TransMilenio buses and taxis weave through the city's arteries, while bikes offer a more intimate way to navigate the bustling streets.

Accommodation options are as diverse as the city itself, from trendy boutique hotels and charming guesthouses to traditional B&Bs and modern Airbnbs. And safety tips are readily available, ensuring a relaxed and worry-free exploration.

Spanish is the language of Bogotá, but don't let that deter you. Basic phrases go a long way, and the warmth of the people will bridge any language gap.

This isn't a city for the faint of heart. Bogotá is a whirlwind, a sensory overload, beautiful chaos that will leave you breathless and begging for more. It's a city that will challenge your preconceptions and rewrite your travel map.

So, come, lose yourself in the vibrant chaos of Bogotá, the city that dances to its own rhythm and wears its contradictions like a crown. Let this emerald jewel of the Andes captivate you, embrace you, and rewrite your definition of adventure.

This is not just a city. This is Bogotá.

And you're invited to dance.

Bogotá Bites

Top Trends and Seasonal Delights for 2024

Bogotá, Colombia's ever-evolving capital, isn't content resting on its laurels of colonial charm and salsa rhythms. This city thrumming with Andean energy is a trendsetter, constantly reinventing itself and offering fresh experiences for the intrepid traveler. So, what's hot in Bogotá right now? Buckle up, amigos, because we're about to dive into the city's coolest corners and seasonal specialties you can't miss:

Urban Adventures:

- *Street Art Safari:* Gone are the days of graffiti as vandalism. Bogotá's street art scene is exploding, transforming walls into canvases for vibrant murals and thought-provoking installations. Get your fill in La Candelaria, Macarena, and Chapinero, where talented artists like Toxicomano and Stinkfish leave their mark. Join a guided tour or grab a map and embark on your own urban safari –

just remember, respect the artwork and the neighborhoods!

- *Hidden Speakeasies:* Forget neon signs and flashing lights. Bogotá's coolest watering holes are tucked away in unassuming buildings, accessed through secret doors or unmarked staircases. Seek out gems like El Grieta in Zona Rosa, where classic cocktails meet an intimate speakeasy vibe, or Candelaria's El Gato Gris, hidden behind a vintage bookstore door.

- *Rooftop Revelry:* Escape the city's buzz and sip cocktails under the Andean sky. Trendy rooftop bars are popping up like wildflowers, offering breathtaking panoramas and vibrant atmospheres. From the chic terrace of El Cielo in Zona G to the bohemian vibes of Macarena's Casa M, each rooftop promises a unique experience.

Foodie Feasts:

- *Farm-to-Table Frenzy:* Forget processed delights, Bogotá's palate is turning towards fresh, local ingredients. Restaurants like Ocal, led by rising star chef Leo Espinosa, source directly from Colombian farms, creating innovative dishes that highlight the country's diverse flavors. Embark on a culinary journey through Colombia's rich terroir, one bite at a time.

- *Vegan Vibes:* Plant-based power is taking Bogotá by storm! Vegan cafes and restaurants are popping up across the city, offering everything from gourmet burgers and succulent pasta to tropical smoothies and decadent desserts. Check out Crudo y Sitio in Chapinero or Vegetariano en Flor in Usaquén for delicious meat-free meals that will leave you wanting more.

- *Coffee Culture Craze:* Colombia is synonymous with coffee, and Bogotá is no exception. Beyond the ubiquitous tinto (strong black coffee), specialty cafes are brewing up a storm. Third-wave coffee shops like Amor Perfecto and Café Cultor roast their beans to perfection, offering pour-overs, cold brews, and nitro coffees that will tantalize your taste buds and fuel your wanderings.

Seasonal Sizzle:

- *Spring Fiesta (March-May):* Bogotá bursts into bloom during spring. Witness the vibrant spectacle of the Festival de las Flores, with parades bursting with color, flower carpets adorning plazas, and the infectious joy of traditional dances. Escape the city buzz to the nearby village of Sopó for their iconic Festival de la Cuchara, a celebration of Colombian cuisine with tastings and cooking demonstrations.

- *Summer Sounds (June-August):* As the city heats up, so does the nightlife. Live music spills out of bars and plazas, with salsa rhythms competing with electronic beats and indie rock tunes. Don't miss the Bogotá Salsa Festival, a whirlwind of workshops, competitions, and open-air dance floors that will have you moving even if you have two left feet.

- *Autumnal Adventures (September-November):* Fall brings harvest season, and Bogotá's markets overflow with fresh produce. Dive into the vibrant La Concordia market, a sensory overload of exotic fruits, colorful vegetables, and fragrant spices. Join a cooking class and learn to whip up local favorites like ajiaco or bandeja paisa, using the season's bounty.

- *Festive Frolic (December-February):* Christmas in Bogotá is an experience like no other. The city transforms into a wonderland of twinkling lights, festive decorations, and traditional celebrations. Attend the Festival de Luces, where entire streets are illuminated with dazzling light displays, or witness the enchanting Nativity scene at Plaza de

Bolívar. Don't forget to indulge in festive treats like buñuelos (deep-fried cheese bread) and natilla (sweetened cream) for a taste of Colombian Christmas magic.

Beyond the City Limits:

- *Coffee Country Escape:* Immerse yourself in the emerald green embrace of Colombia's Coffee Region. Learn the secrets of the perfect cup at a charming hacienda, hike through lush coffee plantations, and enjoy breathtaking mountain views.

- *Amazonian Odyssey:* Embark on an unforgettable adventure into the vibrant heart of the Amazon rainforest. Trek through dense jungle, encounter diverse wildlife and discover ...discover indigenous communities who have called this verdant paradise home for millennia. Experience their traditions, learn about their connection to the land, and witness the awe-inspiring biodiversity of the rainforest firsthand. Remember, responsible tourism is key in such delicate ecosystems, so choose ethical operators and leave nothing but footprints.

Ready to dive into the vibrant chaos of Bogotá and beyond? This city has something for everyone, from adrenaline-pumping adventures to laid-back cultural immersions. So pack your dancing shoes, your adventurous spirit, and an appetite for unforgettable experiences. Bogotá awaits, and it's ready to make you fall head over heels in love with its unique rhythm and captivating charm.

Pro-Tip:

- Bogotá's altitude (2,600 meters) can impact some travelers. Take it slow on arrival, stay hydrated, and avoid strenuous activity on your first day.
- Invest in a good Bogota City Card for discounted entry to museums, attractions, and public transportation.
- Learn a few basic Spanish phrases – it goes a long way in this friendly city.

- Download offline maps and translation apps to ensure smooth navigation around the city.
- Pack comfortable shoes – you'll be doing a lot of walking!
- Carry cash for smaller purchases and street vendors.
- Embrace the unexpected – that's the magic of Bogotá!

Bogotá is more than just a city; it's an experience. Come, lose yourself in its vibrant streets, savor its diverse flavors, and let its infectious energy dance into your soul. This is Bogotá, and you're invited to stay a while, discover its secrets, and create memories that will last a lifetime.

Buen viaje!

Remember, you can tailor it further by adding details about specific seasonal events or attractions that spark your interest. Enjoy exploring Bogotá!

Planning Your Bogotá Adventure

Conquering Chaos with Confidence

Bogotá, Colombia's pulsating capital, is a sensory explosion waiting to be devoured. But beneath the vibrant surface lies a complex city, and navigating its charm can feel like a tango – exhilarating and slightly unpredictable. Fear not, intrepid traveler! With these essential tips, you'll master Bogotá's rhythm and plan a smooth, stylish adventure that's uniquely yours.

Visas and Logistics:

- *Visas:* Most nationalities can enter Colombia visa-free for up to 180 days. Double-check visa requirements for your country of origin before booking your flights.
- *Flights:* Bogotá's El Dorado International Airport (BOG) is well-connected with major airlines. Consider booking in advance during peak seasons (December-January, July-August) for better deals.

- *Currency:* The Colombian peso (COP) is the local currency. ATMs are widely available, but carrying cash (USD or EUR) for smaller purchases is recommended.
- *Travel Insurance:* Invest in comprehensive travel insurance that covers medical emergencies, trip cancellations, and lost luggage.

Accommodations for Every Vibe:

- *Trendy Boutique Hotels:* La Candelaria and Zona Rosa boast stylish hotels with modern amenities and rooftop bars for Instagram-worthy views. Check out Casa Dann Cartagena or Selina Candelaria for a luxurious dose of local flair.
- *Charming Guesthouses:* Macarena and Chapinero offer cozy guesthouses and B&Bs with unique characters and friendly hosts. La Posada del Cielo or Casa Verde offers warm hospitality and a taste of authentic Bogotá life.
- *Modern Airbnbs:* For a home-away-from-home experience, explore trendy neighborhoods like

Chapinero or Usaquén for stylish apartments with fully equipped kitchens and local recommendations from your host.

- *Sustainable Stays:* Eco-conscious travelers can opt for eco-friendly hotels like Casa Legado or Bio Habitat Hotel, which prioritize local materials, energy efficiency, and community engagement.

Transportation Like a Local:

- *TransMilenio:* Bogotá's efficient bus rapid transit system is clean, affordable, and covers most of the city. Download the TransMilenio app for real-time information and route planning.
- *Taxis:* Yellow cabs are abundant and relatively cheap. Negotiate fares beforehand and stick to officially licensed taxis for safety.
- *Uber and Didi:* Ride-hailing apps like Uber and Didi offer convenient alternatives, especially for late-night travel.
- *Bike Sharing:* Bogotá's bike-sharing network, Bicitá, is a fun and eco-friendly

way to explore the city. Download the app, grab a bike, and pedal your way to adventure.

Staying Safe and Savvy:

- *Pickpocketing* is common in crowded areas. Keep valuables close, use money belts, and avoid displaying expensive jewelry.
- Stay vigilant after dark. Stick to well-lit areas and avoid deserted streets.
- Learn basic Spanish phrases. While English is spoken in some tourist areas, basic Spanish goes a long way and opens doors to authentic experiences.
- Bargaining is expected at markets and street vendors. Start with half the asking price and negotiate politely for a fair deal.
- Download offline maps and translation apps. Bogotá's internet connectivity can be patchy, so be prepared with offline resources.
- Dress comfortably and weather appropriately. Pack layers for the unpredictable Andean climate,

comfortable shoes for walking, and a light rain jacket for sudden downpours.

Culture & Connection:

- *Free Walking Tours:* Join a free walking tour to get your bearings, learn about Bogotá's history and culture, and mingle with fellow travelers. Look for reputable companies with local guides.
- *Coffee Culture:* Immerse yourself in Colombia's coffee scene. Sample locally roasted beans at trendy cafes like Amor Perfecto or Cafe Cultor, and take a coffee tour in La Candelaria to learn the bean-to-cup process.
- *Nightlife:* Bogotá's nightlife is legendary. Dance to salsa rhythms in Zona Rosa, sip cocktails on a rooftop bar in Macarena or catch a live music show in Chapinero. Remember, Colombians party late, so adjust your expectations!
- *Local Markets:* Experience the buzz of vibrant markets like La Concordia or Usaquén. Stock up on fresh produce,

souvenirs, and handcrafted treasures, and don't forget to bargain!

- *Volunteer Opportunities:* Contribute to the local community by volunteering at an NGO or orphanage. Several organizations offer short-term programs for travelers who want to make a difference.

Seasonal Delights:

- *Spring (March-May):* Witness the vibrant Festival de las Flores, indulge in fresh harvest at the Festival de la Cuchara, and escape to the Andean countryside for wildflowers and tranquility.
- *Summer (June-August):* Summer (June-August): Join the city's summer salsa fever at the Bogotá Salsa Festival, soak up the sun on a rooftop bar with breathtaking mountain views, and explore nearby towns like Villa de Leyva for colonial charm and outdoor adventures.

- *Autumn (September-November):* Immerse yourself in the harvest season at La Concordia market, learn to cook traditional Colombian dishes in a cooking class, and witness the enchanting Festival de Luces with dazzling light displays throughout the city.
- *Winter (December-February):* Celebrate a magical Christmas in Bogotá with twinkling lights, festive decorations, and traditional celebrations like Nativity scenes and parades. Enjoy local delicacies like buñuelos and natilla for a taste of Colombian Christmas magic.

Tech-Savvy Travelers:

- Download the Bogota City Card: Get discounts on museums, attractions, and public transportation, ensuring a budget-friendly and convenient exploration.
- *Connect to WiFi:* Most cafes, restaurants, and hotels offer free WiFi. Look for the "WiFi Gratis" sign to stay connected.

- *Use mobile apps:* Utilize Bogotá's official transit app for real-time bus information, translation apps for communication, and food delivery apps for culinary convenience.

Remember:

- Bogotá is a walking city. Wear comfortable shoes and be prepared for hills.
- Respect local customs and traditions. Dress modestly at religious sites and avoid sensitive topics like the drug trade.
- Tipping is not expected. A simple "gracias" is sufficient at most restaurants and cafes.
- Support local businesses. Opt for independent shops and cafes over chain stores to contribute to the community.
- Embrace the unpredictable! Bogotá is a city that thrives on spontaneity. Be open to unexpected encounters, detours, and the occasional power outage.

Bogotá is a journey, not a destination. It's a city that challenges your preconceptions, pushes your boundaries, and rewards you with unforgettable experiences. With these tips, you're ready to navigate its vibrant chaos, conquer its charms, and create memories that will forever shimmer with the emerald fire of this captivating Colombian capital. Buen viaje!

Bogotá's Neighborhood Tapestry

Unveiling the City's Diverse Charms

Bogotá is a city woven from countless threads, each neighborhood a distinctive hue in its vibrant tapestry. To truly experience the beating heart of Colombia's capital, venture beyond the tourist trail and immerse yourself in these five unique enclaves, each with its own personality and pulse:

La Candelaria: History meets Hipster

Cobbled streets whisper tales of conquistadors and revolutionaries as you wander through La Candelaria, Bogotá's historic heart. Vibrant murals splash across colonial façades, while quaint plazas buzz with street performers and locals basking in the Andean sun. Explore the Gold Museum, where pre-Columbian treasures glitter like forgotten dreams, or climb Monserrate for panoramic vistas and a colonial church nestled in the clouds. By day, sip coffee in trendy cafes housed in old mansions, browse for handcrafted souvenirs in bohemian stores and learn how to salsa in hidden studios. As dusk paints the city in warm hues, grab a craft beer at a rooftop bar overlooking the twinkling cityscape, or lose yourself in the infectious rhythm of live music spilling from cozy jazz clubs. This neighborhood is a living, breathing museum, where history and hipster trends tango under the watchful gaze of ancient churches.

Zona Rosa: Where Luxury Meets Glitter

Zona Rosa, also known as Zona T, pulsates with the city's upscale heartbeat. High-rise buildings shimmer with designer boutiques like Armani and Dolce & Gabbana, catering to Bogotá's fashionistas. Art galleries showcase contemporary exhibits, while gourmet restaurants like Astrid y Gaston tempt your palate with avant-garde culinary creations. As twilight descends, the district transforms into a playground for the elite. Cocktail bars with velvet sofas and dim lighting become havens for whispered conversations and high-powered deals. Glittering nightclubs throb with electronic beats and salsa rhythms, attracting a well-heeled crowd eager to dance until dawn. But Zona Rosa isn't just for the opulent; its diverse culinary scene offers affordable delights like empanadas and arepas alongside Michelin-starred menus. So, whether you're a window shopper or a nightlife aficionado, Zona Rosa promises a glamorous escape under the city's neon canopy.

Macarena: Bohemian Beatnik Beat

Macarena is a haven for free spirits and creative souls. Independent shops housed in colorful buildings display locally designed fashion, vintage treasures, and handmade crafts. Art galleries offer a platform for emerging artists, while hip cafes with mismatched furniture and eclectic music become impromptu meeting places for artists, musicians, and writers. Wander down leafy streets adorned with street art, each mural a vibrant story whispered onto brick walls. By day, sip a craft latte while reading a poetry book, browse unique jewelry crafted by local artisans, or join a pottery class to unleash your inner creativity. As the sun dips below the rooftops, rooftop bars with panoramic views beckon with artisanal cocktails and indie tunes. Late-night music venues vibrate with live performances, from rock bands to acoustic singer-songwriters, making Macarena a haven for those who love the raw energy of the underground scene.

Chapinero: A Fusion of Old and New

Chapinero is a neighborhood in transition, where traditional houses rub shoulders with trendy co-working spaces and hip cafes. Brick buildings painted in bold colors house craft breweries brewing artisanal beers, while old-school butcher shops share sidewalks with vegetarian restaurants offering organic delights. Explore the iconic "Hippie Park," a green oasis within the urban jungle, and wander through the charming Quinta Camacho neighborhood, known for its colonial mansions and cobbled streets. In the afternoon, grab a bite at a street vendor serving steaming hot ajiaco or join a cooking class to learn the secrets of Colombian cuisine. As night falls, Zona G, a gourmet haven within Chapinero, comes alive with fine-dining restaurants serving exquisite plates under twinkling lights. Later, catch a live music show at a trendy bar or dance to salsa rhythms in a traditional club, experiencing the best of both worlds in this ever-evolving district.

Usaquén: European Elegance with Colombian Flair

Tucked away in the northern reaches of Bogotá lies Usaquén, an upscale neighborhood exuding a distinctly European vibe. Wide, tree-lined avenues and elegant mansions give way to charming plazas and manicured parks. Browse chic boutiques showcasing Colombian and international fashion, or stock up on fresh produce and gourmet goodies at the bustling Usaquén market. Sip on freshly brewed coffee at a terrace cafe while watching families picnic in the Park El Virrey, a green oasis perfect for a leisurely afternoon. On Sundays, the neighborhood transforms into a vibrant handicraft fair, a kaleidoscope of colors and textures where you can find everything from woven alpaca blankets to hand-painted pottery. Usaquén offers a peaceful retreat from the city's buzz, but don't let its elegance fool you. After dark, trendy bars and restaurants come alive with laughter and conversation, offering a sophisticated yet warm atmosphere for a memorable evening.

Bogotá's Treasures Unveiled

Must-See Sights & Experiences for the Curious Traveler

Bogotá is a feast for the senses, where ancient whispers mingle with urban buzz, and iconic landmarks stand proud amidst contemporary energy. To truly grasp the soul of this captivating city, let's delve into five must-see sights and experiences guaranteed to leave you spellbound:

1. El Dorado's Glittering Past: The Gold Museum

Forget King Midas, Bogotá boasts the real treasure trove! The Museo del Oro is a dazzling portal to pre-Columbian civilizations, housing the world's largest collection of pre-Columbian gold artifacts. Witness over 50,000 shimmering pieces, from intricate masks and ceremonial objects to delicate figurines and gleaming nuggets. Each artifact whispers tales of forgotten empires, forgotten rituals, and the extraordinary craftsmanship of ancient peoples. Interactive exhibits and guided tours bring these stories to life, weaving a spell of wonder as you discover the golden threads that connect Bogotá's past to its vibrant present.

2. City Views and Celestial Bliss: Monserrate's Embrace

Ascend to the heavens, Bogotá-style! Monserrate, the iconic mountain overlooking the city, offers breathtaking panoramas for those seeking epic views and spiritual immersion. Cable car your way up, or if you're feeling adventurous, embark on a scenic hike through lush forest trails. At the summit, the colonial Santuario de Monserrate church welcomes you with its serene atmosphere and stunning frescoes. Explore the nearby gardens, bask in the Andean breeze, and witness the city shrink below you like a vibrant mosaic. As dusk paints the sky in fiery hues, stay for the nightly candlelit mass, an ethereal experience that will leave you awestruck.

3. *Whimsical Giants and Sculptural Stories: Botero's Enigmatic World*

Prepare to have your perspective warped and your smile widened at the Fernando Botero Museum. Step into a world where rotund figures dominate canvases and sculptures, their exaggerated proportions injecting humor and thought-provoking questions into everyday life. From the iconic reclining nudes to the playful animal sculptures, Botero's works challenge societal norms and celebrate the beauty of life in all its forms. Explore the museum's collection, delve into the artist's creative process through interactive exhibits, and leave with a new appreciation for the power of art to surprise and delight.

4. Urban Canvas Explosion: La Macarena's Street Art Symphony

Bogotá's streets hold stories, and in La Macarena, they're splashed across walls in murals larger than life. This bohemian enclave is a playground for street artists, transforming buildings into vibrant canvases that captivate and inspire. Join a guided tour to learn about the artists, techniques, and social messages embedded in the artwork, or take a self-guided stroll, letting the urban symphony of colors and textures wash over you. Be sure to bring your camera and your imagination, as each corner promises a new artistic encounter to ignite your creativity.

5. An Oasis of Knowledge and Tranquility: Virgilio Barco Library

Escape the city's buzz and enter a sanctuary of knowledge and architectural beauty at the Virgilio Barco Library. Designed by Colombian architect Rogelio

Salmona, the library itself is a masterpiece, with cascading brick arches, lush indoor gardens, and a tranquil reflecting pool. Inside, immerse yourself in the extensive collection of books, browse through historical documents, or simply relax in the serene atmosphere. Grab a coffee at the on-site cafe, surrounded by literary treasures, and soak in the peaceful energy of this intellectual haven.

These five experiences are just a glimpse into the treasure chest that is Bogotá. From pre-Columbian gold to contemporary art, mountaintop vistas to urban art labyrinths, this city offers endless possibilities for the curious traveler. So, pack your sense of adventure, an open mind, and a healthy dose of wonder, and prepare to be captivated by Bogotá's unique magic.

Bogotá Blooms and Buzzes

Seasonal Delights for Every Traveler

Bogotá, Colombia's vibrant capital, isn't just a city – it's a living calendar packed with seasonal delights waiting to be savored. Whether you crave floral explosions, festive revelry, or cozy winter magic, there's a perfect time to embrace the energy of this captivating city. So, grab your calendar, and let's dive into the seasonal gems Bogotá has to offer:

Springtime Serenade (March-May):

- *Festival de las Flores (April):* Witness Bogotá transform into a floral wonderland! Streets burst with vibrant floats bursting with blooms, colorful parades dance through plazas, and the entire city becomes a symphony of fragrance. Join the flower battle, a playful tradition where revelers shower each other with petals, or admire the intricate flower carpets adorning squares.

- *Semana Santa (Easter Week):* Experience the city's spiritual side during Semana Santa. Witness solemn processions and candlelit vigils, echoing with chants and hymns. Savor traditional dishes like bunuelos (cheese fritters) and natilla (sweet cream) while soaking in the atmosphere of reflection and community.
- *Perfect weather for outdoor adventures:* Springtime welcomes pleasant temperatures and sunshine, making it ideal for exploring Bogotá's green spaces. Hike to the summit of Monserrate, picnic in Parque El Virrey, or bike through La Candelaria's charming streets, enjoying the city's fresh breath.

Summer Sounds and Celebrations (June-August):

- *Independence Day Fiesta (July 20th):* Join the city's patriotic fervor on Independence Day! Parades with dancing troupes and marching bands fill the streets, while concerts and family picnics create a festive atmosphere. Paint your face in the national colors, wave Colombian flags, and immerse yourself in the joyous spirit of celebration.

- *Open-air concerts and cultural events:* Summer nights come alive with vibrant cultural offerings. Catch an open-air concert in Usaquén Park, watch a play under the stars in La Candelaria, or savor classical music performances in historic churches. Don't miss the Bogotá Fashion Week in August, showcasing the city's hottest design talent.

- *Mountain escapes and outdoor adventures:* As the city heats up, seek refuge in the cool embrace of nearby mountain towns. Explore the charming village of Villa de Leyva, go white-water rafting in Suesca, or hike through the emerald-green foothills of the Andes.

Autumnal Bounty and Cultural Treasures (September-November):

- *Harvest season bounty:* Autumn paints Bogotá's markets with the vibrant colors of fresh produce. Immerse yourself in the chaotic energy of La Concordia market, sampling exotic fruits like lulo and guayaba, or stock up on seasonal vegetables for a taste of Colombian home cooking. Don't forget to join the annual Festival de la Cuchara in Sopó, a celebration of local cuisine with tastings and cooking demonstrations.

- *Museum hopping and cultural immersion:* Bogotá's cultural scene takes center stage in autumn. Explore the city's many museums, from the renowned Gold Museum to the Botero Museum's humorous sculptures. Attend a theater performance, catch a film festival, or join a literary event and soak in the city's intellectual buzz.

- *Cozy coffee culture and local festivals:* As the evenings turn cooler, find warmth and comfort in Bogotá's vibrant coffee scene. Sip on a steaming cup of locally roasted brew in a trendy cafe, linger over a book in a cozy bookshop, and savor the city's laid-back charm. Be sure to check out local festivals like the Festival de

Teatro Callejero (Street Theater Festival) for a dose of creative energy.

Winter Wonderland and Sparkling Celebrations (December-February):

- *Enchanted Christmas:* Bogotá transforms into a magical wonderland during Christmas. Twinkling lights drape streets, nativity scenes adorn plazas, and festive music fills the air. Sip on hot chocolate at a Christmas market, witness the enchanting Nochebuena (Christmas Eve) celebrations, and indulge in traditional treats like buñuelos and natilla.
- *New Year's Eve festivities:* Ring in the New Year with vibrant parties and unforgettable experiences. Dance to salsa rhythms in Zona Rosa, join a rooftop celebration overlooking the city lights or follow the traditional burning of muñeco year-end ritual for good luck in the year ahead.

- *Cozy nights and cultural retreats:* Escape the winter chill and find warmth in Bogotá's many cafes, restaurants, and cultural venues. Enjoy a live jazz performance in a dimly lit bar, curl up with a book in a cozy fireplace-warmed bookstore, or indulge in a spa treatment to pamper yourself before the new year starts.

This is just a taste of the seasonal delights that await you in Bogotá. Remember, Colombia's diverse climate and cultural calendar offer something special for every traveler, no matter when you choose to visit.

Bogotá Bites

A Foodie's Adventure in the Culinary Canopy of Colombia

Bogotá is a city that thrums with a heartbeat of its own, and that rhythm? It's fueled by the tantalizing melodies of a vibrant, diverse food scene. Whether you're a seasoned gourmand or a curious culinary explorer, prepare to be seduced by the aromatic symphony of flavors that awaits in this captivating Colombian capital. Let's dive into the irresistible delights that will awaken your taste buds and make your Bogotá adventure a mouthwatering journey:

1. A Taste of Tradition: Colombian Cuisine Delights

- *Ajiaco Santafereño*: The undisputed queen of Bogotá's culinary court, this hearty chicken stew is a symphony of textures and flavors. Three types of potatoes mingle with juicy chicken, creamy avocado, and the star ingredient

– guascas, a fragrant herb that provides a unique, floral touch. Each bite is a warm hug that whispers tales of Colombian home cooking.

- *Bandeja Paisa:* Forget dainty portions – this dish is a carnivore's dream. Picture a platter overflowing with grilled meats like chorizo, steak, and pork belly, alongside fried eggs, fluffy rice, beans, sweet plantains, and fresh avocado. It's a fiesta of flavors, guaranteed to leave you satisfied and ready for a siesta.

- *Arepas:* These addictive cornmeal flatbreads are the chameleon of Colombian cuisine. Crispy on the outside, soft and chewy within, they can be enjoyed plain, stuffed with cheese, meat, or vegetables, or dipped in delicious sauces. From breakfast to late-night snacks, arepas are a ubiquitous companion on your Bogotá journey.

2. *Around the World in a Bite: International Flavors Abound*

Bogotá's cosmopolitan spirit translates to its culinary landscape. Craving fresh sushi? Zona

Rosa boasts sleek Japanese restaurants with melt-in-your-mouth sashimi and delicately crafted makis. Italian cravings can be appeased in Chapinero, where cozy trattorias serve up al dente pastas and wood-fired pizzas with authentic mozzarella. For a taste of Peru, head to Usaquén, where ceviche masters dish up vibrant seafood marinated in citrusy perfection.

3. Street Food for the Adventurous Soul:

No exploration of Bogotá would be complete without venturing into the world of street food. Don't let the casual setting fool you – these vibrant vendors are culinary alchemists, transforming simple ingredients into flavor bombs. Devour steaming empanadas with savory fillings, indulge in papas rellenas (stuffed potatoes) oozing with cheese and aji sauce, or grab a cob of choclo con queso (corn with cheese) for a warm, sweet streetside treat.

4. Coffee Culture: Fueling Your Footsteps with Colombian Brews

Bogotá is not just a city – it's a coffee capital. Forget instant brews and Starbucks chains – here, coffee is an art form, meticulously roasted and brewed to perfection. Wander into trendy cafes like Amor Perfecto or Cafe Cultor, where the air hums with conversations and the aroma of freshly roasted beans hangs heavy like a fragrant fog. Sip on single-origin pour-overs, savor cold brews crafted with precision, or try a traditional tinto (strong black coffee) for a jolt of energy to propel your Bogotá adventure.

5. Nightlife & Entertainment: A Feast for the Senses After Dark

As the sun dips below the Andean peaks, Bogotá's culinary scene shifts gears, transforming into a vibrant symphony of nightlife and entertainment. Salsa your way through the night in Zona Rosa, where clubs pulsate with infectious rhythms and dancers showcase their fiery footwork. Rooftop bars in Macarena offer breathtaking city views and sophisticated cocktails, while live music venues in La Candelaria serenade you with everything from indie rock to traditional Colombian tunes. Whether you're seeking a late-night bite, a dance floor fiesta, or a soulful musical experience, Bogotá's nightlife promises a feast for the senses that will keep you buzzing until dawn.

This is just a glimpse into the culinary wonderland that awaits you in Bogotá. From traditional delights to international flavors, street food adventures to coffee-fueled explorations, and late-night feasts to vibrant entertainment, the city's culinary landscape is a kaleidoscope of taste and experience. So, pack your appetite, ditch the guidebook, and let your nose lead you through the fragrant streets of Bogotá. This vibrant foodie paradise promises to seduce your taste buds, tickle your senses, and leave you with memories that will linger long after you leave. Buen provecho!

Beyond Bogotá's Buzz

Adventures Await in Colombia's Diverse Landscape

Bogotá offers an intoxicating blend of vibrant energy, historical treasures, and captivating cuisine. But beyond the city limits, Colombia's diverse landscape unfolds, revealing breathtaking natural wonders, charming towns, and unique cultural experiences waiting to be discovered. So, pack your sense of adventure, and let's explore some unforgettable day trips from Bogotá:

1. Zipaquirá: Where Faith Takes Root in Salt (1.5 hours)

Descend into the heart of a mountain at the Zipaquirá Salt Cathedral, an awe-inspiring architectural marvel carved from rock salt. This subterranean cathedral, considered one of the wonders of Colombia, is a testament to human faith and artistry. Witness the luminous cross bathed in colored spotlights, wander through the Stations of the Cross, and marvel at the cavernous nave, all sculpted from the earth's bounty.

2. Guatavita: A Dive into Legend and Emerald Waters (2 hours)

Legend whispers of El Dorado, the mythical city of gold, said to be hidden in a sacred lake. While you might not find golden treasures, the emerald-green Guatavita Lake offers a captivating glimpse into pre-Columbian history and stunning Andean scenery. Hike to the lake's rim, learn about the Muisca ritual of El Dorado and the legend of gold offerings, and soak in the mystical atmosphere of this ancient site.

3. Villa de Leyva: Colonial Charm with a Modern Twist (3 hours)

Step back in time to the cobbled streets and whitewashed houses of Villa de Leyva, a charming colonial town nestled in the Andean foothills. Stroll through the main square, Plaza Mayor, admire the historic churches and colorful buildings, and indulge in delicious local cuisine at cozy cafes. Explore the nearby paleontological museum, discover fossils that whisper tales of ancient creatures, and soak in the laid-back atmosphere of this timeless gem.

4. Coffee Adventure: From Bean to Bliss in the Andes (2-3 days)

Immerse yourself in the heart and soul of Colombia's coffee culture with a visit to a traditional hacienda in the Andes mountains. Learn about the bean-to-cup process, from picking ripe cherries to roasting and brewing the perfect cup. Stay in a rustic hacienda, savor locally grown food, and wake up to breathtaking mountain views. Participate in a coffee workshop, learn the secrets of brewing like a pro, and savor the rich aroma and complex flavors of freshly roasted Colombian coffee.

5. Amazonian Odyssey: Embrace the Lush Embrace of the Rainforest (5-7 days)

For those seeking an unforgettable adventure, venture into the emerald embrace of the Colombian Amazon rainforest. From Leticia, embark on a boat trip down the Rio Amazonas, spot pink dolphins, and exotic birds, and witness the diversity of this vital ecosystem.

Learn about indigenous communities and their sustainable practices, hike through the lush jungle, and spend a night under the star-studded Amazonian sky. This transformative experience will connect you to the raw beauty of nature and leave you with a deep respect for the rainforest's delicate balance.

These are just a few possibilities waiting to be explored beyond the buzz of Bogotá. Whether you're seeking historical wonders, natural beauty, or cultural immersion, Colombia's diverse landscape offers experiences that will stay with you long after your journey ends. So, pack your bags, choose your adventure, and prepare to be enchanted by the magic that lies beyond Bogotá's city limits.

Remember, this is just a starting point. You can tailor these descriptions to include specific details about current festivals or events in these towns, recommended restaurants or cafes, or specific activities you can partake in, creating a personalized itinerary for your adventure beyond Bogotá. Buen viaje!

Conquering Bogotá

Navigating the Buzz with Ease

Bogotá, a vibrant tapestry of history, culture, and urban energy, welcomes you with open arms. But before you dive into its captivating chaos, let's equip you with the practical know-how to navigate this enthralling city like a seasoned Bogotano.

Taming the Transit:

- TransMilenio: Bogotá's lifeline is its efficient bus rapid transit system, TransMilenio. Purchase a Tarjeta Tu Llave at designated stations or kiosks, hop on the red buses, and zip across the city with ease. Download the TransMilenio app for real-time bus information and route planning.
- Taxis: Yellow taxis are readily available, metered fares ensure transparency, and Uber operates for added convenience. Negotiate fares for white taxis beforehand. Tip the driver 10% of the fare.

- Biking: Bogotá boasts an extensive network of bike lanes. Rent a bike from Ciclovia or private shops and join the growing community of eco-conscious commuters. Helmets are mandatory, and certain areas are best explored on two wheels.
- On Foot: The best way to savor the city's atmosphere is on foot. Explore La Candelaria's cobbled streets, wander through Usaquén's tree-lined avenues, and soak in the local vibe. Just be mindful of traffic and keep valuables secure.

Finding Your Urban Nest:
- Trendy Hotels: Zona Rosa and Zona T offer sleek, modern hotels with high-end amenities and rooftop bars boasting city views. Expect contemporary design and a chic atmosphere.
- Boutique Guesthouses: La Candelaria and Macarena are home to charming guest houses housed in colonial buildings. Enjoy personalized service,

rooftop terraces, and a true feel for the city's history.

- Airbnbs: For a local experience, explore the diverse neighborhoods through unique Airbnb stays. Apartments, lofts, and even cozy casitas offer a glimpse into local life and budget-friendly options.

Safety First:

- General precautions: Keep an eye on your belongings, especially in crowded areas. Avoid displaying valuables openly. Late-night strolls are best tackled with company.
- Pickpockets: be wary in crowded areas like TransMilenio stations and popular attractions. Keep wallets and phones in secure pockets or money belts.
- Taxis: Only use licensed taxis or ride-sharing apps like Uber. Agree on fares beforehand and avoid unmarked vehicles.
- Emergency Numbers: 123 for police, 112 for medical emergencies, and 116 for fire department. Dial +57 (1) if calling from outside Colombia.

Breaking the Language Barrier:
While English is gaining traction, basic Spanish goes a long way. Here are some helpful phrases:

- Hola/Buenas tardes/Buenas noches: Hello/Good afternoon/Good evening
- Gracias: Thank you
- De nada: You're welcome
- Hablas inglés?: Do you speak English?
- Me llamo _____: My name is _____
- Cuánto cuesta?: How much is it?
- Dónde está el baño?: Where is the bathroom?
- Necesito ayuda: I need help

Download translation apps and carry a phrasebook for extra support. Don't be afraid to use your hands and smile – Bogotanos are friendly and willing to help.

With these practical tips in your pocket, Bogotá's vibrant tapestry awaits your exploration. Embrace the chaos, navigate the energy, and conquer the city with confidence. Buen viaje!

Remember, this is just a starting point. You can personalize this section by adding information about specific festivals or events happening during your visit, recommended neighborhoods for accommodation based on your preferences, or detailed safety tips for certain areas. Make it your own Bogotá guide!

Bogotá Beyond the Basics

Bonus Tips for Navigating Your Colombian Adventure

1. Seasonal Solutions for Urban Adventurers:

- *Spring Blossoms and Showers (March-May):* Pack an umbrella and lightweight rain gear for occasional showers. Be aware of potential flower allergies during the Festival de las Flores. Consider booking accommodations in advance, as many events draw crowds.
- *Summer Sun and Celebrations (June-August):* Sunscreen and sunglasses are essential for sunny days. During Independence Day celebrations, wear comfortable shoes for parades and expect street closures in central areas. Book mountain escapes early, as these become popular holiday destinations.
- *Autumnal Bounty and Cultural Buzz (September-November):* Enjoy the

pleasant weather and outdoor activities. If attending the Festival de la Cuchara, bring cash to try local delicacies. Museums might experience higher visitor numbers during cultural events, so plan your visits accordingly.

- *Winter Magic and Festive Twinkle (December-February):* Pack warm layers for cooler evenings and potential rain showers. Be prepared for larger crowds and higher prices during Christmas and New Year's celebrations. Consider booking Christmas events and dinners well in advance to avoid disappointment.

2. Sports Spectatorship and Participation:

- *Football (Soccer):* Colombia's national obsession! Catch a game at the Estadio El Campín or watch local matches in plazas and bars. Don your yellow jersey and join the passionate chants.
- *Cycling:* Get swept up in the excitement of the Vuelta a Colombia, a prestigious annual cycling race. Rent a bike and join

the Ciclovia Sundays for a car-free city exploration.

- *Tejo:* This traditional game involves throwing objects at targets filled with gunpowder. Witness the local spirit at Tejo bars, or grab a friend and try your hand at this unique sport.
- *Hiking and Climbing:* Explore the Colombian Andes with various treks and climbing routes for all levels. Hike to Monserrate for panoramic views, or challenge yourself on the Nevado del Huila summit.

3. Job Opportunities: Finding Your Niche in La Bella Patria:

- *Teaching English:* Qualified teachers are in demand, especially in private language schools and universities. TEFL or TESOL certifications are beneficial.
- *Technology and Digital Marketing:* Colombia's tech scene is booming. Developers, programmers, and digital marketers can find exciting opportunities in various industries.

- *Tourism and Hospitality:* From tour guides and hotel managers to travel bloggers and social media influencers, the tourism sector offers diverse opportunities for passionate individuals.
- *Entrepreneurship:* Colombia encourages startups and small businesses. If you have a unique idea and entrepreneurial spirit, Bogotá offers the right ecosystem to make it flourish.

4. A Culinary Tour de Force: Best Bites Beyond Ajiaco:

- *Arepas con Hogao:* Crispy arepas slathered with a vibrant tomato and onion sauce, a simple yet addictive street food delight.
- *Sancocho:* This hearty stew, with variations across the country, combines meat, vegetables, and plantains for a delicious and comforting meal.
- *Empanadas de Piñon:* Delectable pastries stuffed with juicy ground beef and pine nuts, a unique Colombian twist on the classic empanada.

- *Postres de Frutas:* Tropical fruits like passion fruit, guava, and mango shine in refreshing desserts like sorbetes, gelatinas, and fruit salads.
- *Ceviche:* Though originating in Peru, Colombian ceviche adds its own flair, using fresh seafood marinated in citrus juices and coconut milk, often served with crunchy patacones (fried plantains).

Remember, this is just a glimpse into the vast world of Colombian cuisine. Explore local markets, try family recipes at small restaurants, and embrace the adventurous spirit of Colombian food. You might just discover your new favorite dish!

These bonus tips offer a deeper dive into different aspects of your Colombian adventure, preparing you for various situations and enticing you with exciting possibilities. Tailor them to your specific interests and travel plans, making your Bogotá experience truly unforgettable. Buen viaje!

Bogotá Beyond the Guidebooks

Unveiling Hidden Gems and Sustainable Escapes

Bogotá, a city teeming with energy and history, also harbors hidden gems and off-the-beaten-path experiences for the adventurous traveler. Embrace the spirit of discovery and venture beyond the tourist trail to uncover these secret treasures:

1. Hidden Gems for the Curious:

- *Casa del Poeta:* This 17th-century colonial mansion, once home to renowned poet Luis Carlos López, invites you on a journey through time. Explore its charming courtyard, browse the literary collection, and immerse yourself in Colombian poetry's rich heritage.
- *La Candelaria Graffiti Scene:* Wander the backstreets of La Candelaria and discover a vibrant tapestry of street art. From social commentary to playful murals, each piece tells a story, offering a

glimpse into the city's soul. Join a guided tour or lose yourself in the artistic labyrinth, letting the walls whisper tales of local artists and hidden meanings.

- *Parque Bavaria:* Escape the urban buzz and enter an oasis of nature at Parque Bavaria. Hike through lush trails, spot hummingbirds and butterflies, and unwind by the tranquil lake. Pack a picnic and enjoy a peaceful afternoon amid the city's green heart.

- *Mercado de las Pulgas de Usaquén:* Hunt for treasures at this flea market overflowing with vintage finds, handicrafts, and local curiosities. Haggle for quirky souvenirs, discover hidden gems from Bogotá's past, and soak in the lively atmosphere.

2. Sustainable Travel: Treading Lightly in La Bella Patria:

- *Eco-friendly transportation:* Opt for cycling, TransMilenio, or walking within the city. For day trips, choose responsible tour operators that prioritize sustainable practices and support local communities.

- *Accommodation with a conscience:* Stay in eco-friendly hotels or glamping sites committed to conservation efforts and minimizing their environmental impact.
- *Support local businesses:* Choose markets over supermarkets, opt for street food stalls over chain restaurants, and purchase souvenirs from local artisans to boost the local economy and reduce your carbon footprint.
- *Respecting the environment:* Be mindful of water usage, avoid littering, and participate in clean-up initiatives if you wish. Remember, responsible tourism starts with small steps and makes a big difference.

3. Packing Smart for a Stylish Bogotá Adventure:

- *Spring (March-May):* Light, breathable clothing with layers for occasional showers. Pack a waterproof jacket and comfortable shoes for exploring. A vibrant scarf can add a pop of color and double as a sunshade.

- *Summer (June-August):* Light clothing for sunny days, with a hat and sunglasses for protection. Pack comfortable footwear for walking and exploring, and consider a light rain jacket for sudden showers.
- *Autumn (September-November):* Pack for milder temperatures and layering options. Comfortable shoes for walking and exploring are essential. An umbrella is recommended for potential rain showers.
- *Winter (December-February):* Pack warmer layers for cooler evenings and potential rain. Comfortable shoes for walking and exploring are a must. Consider a light rain jacket and an umbrella for the unpredictable weather.
-

Remember, these are just starting points. Adjust your packing list based on your specific activities and planned excursions. Embrace the vibrant colors of Colombian fashion, but pack versatile pieces that can be easily mixed and matched to create stylish outfits for your Bogotá adventure.

With these hidden gems, sustainable tips, and packing advice, you're ready to delve deeper into Bogotá's essence and create a truly unforgettable Colombian experience. Buen viaje!

Bogotá: Where Rhythms Collide and Hearts Take Flight

Bogotá, a city that pulsates with life, whispers tales of history and explodes with vibrant colors, transcends a mere travel destination. It's a symphony of experiences, a kaleidoscope of flavors, and a canvas splashed with the bold hues of the human spirit. From the captivating chaos of La Candelaria to the serene embrace of the Andes, from the rhythmic salsa beats to the intoxicating aroma of freshly roasted coffee, Bogotá awakens your senses and invites you to dance to its unique melody.

This urban symphony isn't just for seasoned travelers or intrepid explorers; it welcomes everyone with open arms and a mischievous wink. Whether you crave historical treasures or contemporary thrills, culinary escapades, or cultural immersion, Bogotá weaves a tapestry of experiences to suit your every desire.

This guide merely whispers the secrets of this alluring city; it's just a stepping stone on your path to creating your own Bogotá story. Dive into the heart of its bustling markets, lose yourself in the maze of winding streets, savor the symphony of flavors on your tongue, and let the infectious laughter of its people fill your soul. In the shadow of Monserrate, beneath the starry Andean sky, you might just find yourself falling in love with the rhythm of Bogotá, a love story written in the language of experience, whispered in the wind, and etched in the memories you take home.

So, pack your sense of adventure, unleash your inner salsa dancer, and prepare to be seduced by the intoxicating magic of Bogotá. This city isn't just a destination; it's a journey that awaits with open arms, ready to leave you breathless, inspired, and forever changed. Buen viaje, queridos viajeros, and may your Bogotá story be vibrant, unforgettable, and uniquely yours.

Remember, this is just a starting point. You can personalize this conclusion by adding a specific anecdote or reflection from your own experience with Bogotá, a call to action for readers to plan their own adventure or a final heartfelt message about the city's magic. Make it your own send-off to the City of Rhythms, ensuring your Bogotá experience stays with you long after you bid farewell.

Made in the USA
Monee, IL
29 October 2024